ABUNDANTLY

Inspiration and Guidance for Daily Living

A *Jesus in My Pocket* Book

Eye has not seen, nor ear heard,
Nor have entered into the heart of man
The things which God has prepared for
those who love Him.

1 Corinthians 2:9

Thomas Nelson Publishers
Nashville

Living Abundantly
Inspiration and Guidance for Daily Living
A *Jesus in My Pocket* Book

Jesus in My Pocket Ministries
PMB #327
6632 Telegraph Road
Bloomfield, MI 48301

Printed in Mexico
1 2 3 4 5 6 . . . 04 03 02 01 00 99

Jesus is the source of my abundance...

When I make my requests known to Him with thanksgiving, I never doubt anything but a perfect outcome.

God's Word says...

He who did not spare His own Son, but delivered Him up for us all, how shall He not with Him also freely give us all things?

Romans 8:32

Just for You

Jesus in My Pocket

Fold Here

FROM: ____________________

TO: ____________________

____

Jesus is the source of my abundance...

Throughout this day I will remind myself to count my blessings, which is another way to focus on the Lord's abundance in my life, instead of focusing on what is lacking.

God's Word says...

Oh, that men would give thanks to the
LORD for His goodness,
And for His wonderful works to the
children of men!
For He satisfies the longing soul,
And fills the hungry with goodness.

Psalm 107:8-9

Just for You

Jesus in My Pocket

Fold Here

FROM: ______________

TO: ______________

____

Jesus is the source of my abundance...

I accept any gift offered to me as the spirit of abundance, whether it is a hello from the bus driver or a smile from my child. Then I pass on the gift of abundance by smiling at the next person I see.

God's Word says...

Give, and it will be given to you: good measure, pressed down, shaken together, and running over will be put into your bosom. For with the same measure that you use, it will be measured back to you.

Luke 6:38

Just for You

Jesus in My Pocket

Fold Here

FROM: ____________________

TO: ____________________

____

Jesus is the source of my abundance...

The transportation I use today is another way Jesus has provided for me. Even my feet are His creation, taking me where I need to go.

God's Word says...

Every good gift and every perfect gift is from above, and comes down from the Father of lights, with whom there is no variation or shadow of turning.

James 1:17

Just for You

Jesus in My Pocket

Fold Here

FROM: ____________________

TO: ____________________

____

Jesus is the source of my abundance...

Competition, opposition, and failure are not a threat to me. I believe in God's goodness and His promise to care for me in life.

God's Word says...

Wait on the LORD,

And keep His way,

And He shall exalt you to inherit the land.

Psalm 37:34

Just for You

Jesus in My Pocket

Fold Here

FROM: ______________________

TO: ______________________

____

Jesus is the source of my abundance...

With Him at my side I need not worry about what might happen tomorrow, nor focus on what I lack. Instead, I will focus on the goodness and provision the Lord has promised for me today.

God's Word says...

Therefore do not worry about tomorrow, for tomorrow will worry about its own things. Sufficient for the day is its own trouble.

Matthew 6:34

Jesus in My Pocket

Just for You

Fold Here

FROM: ____________________

TO: ____________________

____

Jesus is the source of my abundance...

I have faith in the abundance of the Lord, just as I have faith in His presence in my life. When I am doubtful, I ask for strength, and I open my heart to His gifts and generosity.

God's Word says...

"Bring all the tithes into the storehouse. . .
And try Me now in this,"
Says the LORD of hosts,
"If I will not open for you the windows of heaven
And pour out for you such blessing
That there will not be room enough to receive it."

Malachi 3:10

Jesus in My Pocket

Just for You

Fold Here

FROM: ____________________

TO: ____________________

____

Jesus is the source of my abundance...

Whatever food I eat today—my morning toast, my bedtime snack—all comes from the goodness that Jesus has provided for me. I acknowledge His abundance with every meal.

God's Word says...

Therefore, whether you eat or drink, or whatever you do, do all to the glory of God.

1 Corinthians 10:31

Just for You

Jesus in My Pocket

Fold Here

FROM: ______________

TO: ______________

____

Jesus is the source of my abundance...

Because I know Jesus will never desert me, I fear no evil, and I fear no lack—whether it be time, money, love, or creative inspiration.

God's Word says...

Oh, fear the LORD, you His saints!
There is no want to those who fear Him.
The young lions lack and suffer hunger;
But those who seek the LORD shall not
lack any good thing.

Psalm 34:9-10

Just for You

Jesus in My Pocket

Fold Here

FROM: ____________

TO: ____________

____

Jesus is the source of my abundance...

God can only do for me what He can do through me, so I keep myself open and receptive to His plan. I know that every moment He is providing for me.

God's Word says...

He does not withdraw His eyes from the
righteous; . . .
If they obey and serve Him,
They shall spend their days in prosperity,
And their years in pleasures.

Job 36:7, 11

Jesus in My Pocket

Just for You

Fold Here

FROM: ____________

TO: ____________

____

Jesus is the source of my abundance...

I shall not look to my spouse, my parents, my employer, or even myself to provide all I need. Instead, I will keep my focus on God, and know that He is always the ultimate provider.

God's Word says...

For the LORD God is a sun and shield;
The LORD will give grace and glory;
No good thing will He withhold
From those who walk uprightly.

Psalm 84:11

Just for You

Jesus in My Pocket

Fold Here

FROM: ____________

TO: ____________

____

Jesus is the source of my abundance...

Believing in Him and thanking Him are my directives from God. As long as I am thanking Him with all my heart, I am showing that I believe He is there for me.

God's Word says...

He did what was good and right and true before the LORD his God. And in every work that he began in the service of the house of God, in the law and in the commandment, to seek his God, he did it with all his heart. So he prospered.

2 Chronicles 31:20-21

Just for You

Jesus in My Pocket

Fold Here

FROM: ____________

TO: ____________

____

Jesus is the source of my abundance...

As I begin my work today, I will remember that the generosity of the Lord has provided me with a source of income. If I don't always enjoy what I do for a living, I will focus my attention on how I can make a change.

God's Word says...

Better is a little with righteousness,
Than vast revenues without justice.

Proverbs 16:8

Just for You

Jesus in My Pocket

Fold Here

FROM: ______________

TO: ______________

____

Jesus is the source of my abundance...

I have complete faith in Jesus' abundance. Even if I am not living in my ideal surroundings, if my clothes seem out of style or my furniture worn, I know in my heart that I am rich—because Jesus loves me—and my faith grows.

God's Word says...

In the day of prosperity be joyful,
But in the day of adversity consider:
Surely God has appointed the one as well
as the other,
So that man can find out nothing that will
come after him.

Ecclesiastes 7:14

Jesus in My Pocket

Just for You

Fold Here

FROM: ______________

TO: ______________

____

Jesus is the source of my abundance...

I see Jesus' abundance in my family and friends. The people in my life are all a part of the fabric of my existence, threads of friendship and love from the Lord, and I treat them with respect and kindness.

God's Word says...

The blessing of the LORD makes one rich,
And He adds no sorrow with it.

Proverbs 10:22

Just for You

Jesus in My Pocket

Fold Here

FROM: ____________________

TO: ____________________

____

Jesus is the source of my abundance...

If I truly believe in the infinite power of God, I will not lack for anything. My material needs and my spiritual needs are all part of Jesus' promise to care for me.

God's Word says...

Oh, taste and see that the LORD is good;
Blessed is the man who trusts in Him!
Oh, fear the LORD, you His saints!
There is no want to those who fear Him.

Psalm 34:8-9

Just for You

Jesus in My Pocket

Fold Here

FROM: ______________

TO: ______________

____

Jesus is the source of my abundance...

As long as I truly accept His divine presence, I can stop relying on the material world to provide for me, and I can begin to look to God for all He has promised me.

God's Word says...

Abide in Me, and I in you. As the branch cannot bear fruit of itself, unless it abides in the vine, neither can you, unless you abide in Me. . . . If you abide in Me, and My words abide in you, you will ask what you desire, and it shall be done for you.

John 15:4, 7

Jesus in My Pocket

Just for You

Fold Here

FROM: ______________

TO: ______________

____

Jesus is the source of my abundance...

I feel His abundance when a child hugs me. Knowing Jesus cared deeply about little children, I feel His presence in their arms, and I permit His love to flow through them into me.

God's Word says...

Therefore whoever humbles himself as this little child is the greatest in the kingdom of heaven. Whoever receives one little child like this in My name receives Me.

Matthew 18:4

Jesus in My Pocket

Just for You

Fold Here

FROM: ____________________

TO: ____________________

____

Jesus is the source of my abundance...

I accept all of His gifts, especially the morning sun. As I embrace a new day and a new plan, I remember that just as Jesus gave me life, He also gave me the morning sun.

God's Word says...

Your sun shall no longer go down,
Nor shall your moon withdraw itself;
For the LORD will be your everlasting light,
And the days of your mourning shall be ended.

Isaiah 60:20

Jesus in My Pocket

Just for You

Fold Here

FROM: ________________

TO: ________________

____

Jesus is the source of my abundance...

When I accept the gifts of His abundance, I am not poor, I am not limited, and I am not miserable. All things are possible through Him as I keep my heart and mind focused on the Lord.

God's Word says...

The poor and needy seek water, but there
is none.
Their tongues fail for thirst,
I, the LORD, will hear them;
I, the God of Israel, will not forsake them.

Isaiah 41:17

Just for You

Jesus in My Pocket

Fold Here

FROM: ________________

TO: ________________

____

Jesus is the source of my abundance...

To have what I want, to do as I wish, to become what I will, I must banish all thoughts of failure, have faith in God, and rely on the one power I know will never fail me—the power of God's love.

God's Word says...

Now faith is the substance of things hoped for, the evidence of things not seen. . . . But without faith it is impossible to please Him, for he who comes to God must believe that He is, and that He is a rewarder of those who diligently seek Him.

Hebrews 11:1, 6

Just for You

Jesus in My Pocket

Fold Here

FROM: ____________________

TO: ____________________

____

Jesus is the source of my abundance...

I recognize His abundance in the people He brings into my life. I welcome those who are uplifting and encouraging. I pray for those who are negative and pessimistic.

God's Word says...

Honor all people. Love the brotherhood. Fear God. Honor the king.

1 Peter 2:17

Just for You

Jesus in My Pocket

Fold Here

FROM: ________________

TO: ________________

____

Jesus is the source of my abundance...

I will practice honesty and goodness to all those around me. I will deal courteously with my family, friends and coworkers, and they will return the same kindness and respect to me.

God's Word says...

But sanctify the Lord God in your hearts, and always be ready to give a defense to everyone who asks you a reason for the hope that is in you, with meekness and fear.

1 Peter 3:15

Jesus in My Pocket

Just for You

Fold Here

FROM: ______________

TO: ______________

____

Jesus is the source of my abundance...

As long as I trust in the Lord, His abundance comes to me. I accept His internal spark of inspiration, listen for divine intervention, then act confidently.

God's Word says...

And we know that all things work together for good to those who love God, to those who are the called according to His purpose.

Romans 8:28

Just for You

Jesus in My Pocket

Fold Here

FROM: ____________________

TO: ____________________

____

Jesus is the source of my abundance...

The power of choice is one of God's greatest gifts to me. I will choose to keep my thoughts focused on prosperity, success, and abundance by meditating on God's Word.

God's Word says...

This Book of the Law shall not depart from your mouth, but you shall meditate in it day and night, that you may observe to do according to all that is written in it. For then you will make your way prosperous, and then you will have good success.

Joshua 1:8

Jesus in My Pocket

Just for You

Fold Here

FROM: ____________

TO: ____________

____

Jesus is the source of my abundance...

I see abundance everywhere I look—in my kitchen, in the sanctuary of my bedroom, in my backyard. Everything I possess is a symbol of Jesus' love for me.

God's Word says...

Go, eat your bread with joy,
And drink your wine with a merry heart;
For God has already accepted your works.

Ecclesiastes 9:7

Jesus in My Pocket

Just for You

Fold Here

FROM: ____________________

TO: ____________________

____

Jesus is the source of my abundance...

I believe I will have all that I need for this day. As I pray, "Give us this day our daily bread," I will remember that I only need to think about today, and I know God will provide for me if I trust in Him.

God's Word says...

The LORD is my shepherd;

I shall not want.

He makes me lie down in green pastures;

He leads me beside the still waters.

He restores my soul;

He leads me in the paths of righteousness

For His name's sake.

Psalm 23:1-3

Just for You

Jesus in My Pocket

Fold Here

FROM: ______________

TO: ______________

____

Jesus is the source of my abundance...

I accept His gift of abundance willingly and thankfully. I will not constantly ask for more, or complain about what I feel is a meager portion. I will keep in mind that Jesus will provide exactly what I need at exactly the right time.

God's Word says...

Now godliness with contentment is great gain. For we brought nothing into this world, and it is certain we can carry nothing out. And having food and clothing, with these we shall be content.

1 Timothy 6:6-8

Jesus in My Pocket

Just for You

Fold Here

FROM: ____________________

TO: ____________________

____

Jesus is the source of my abundance...

The very air I breathe is a gift from the Lord. I need not question why He is so generous and loving. I need only thank Him continually.

God's Word says...

And whatever you do in word or deed, do all in the name of the Lord Jesus, giving thanks to God the Father through Him.

Colossians 3:17

Jesus in My Pocket

Just for You

Fold Here

FROM: ____________________

TO: ____________________

____

Jesus is the source of my abundance...

I will live richly and fully today. I will take every action to make abundance my reality. Boredom is never present in my active life.

God's Word says...

Blessed are those who do His commandments, that they may have the right to the tree of life.

Revelation 22:14

Just for You

Jesus in My Pocket

Fold Here

FROM: ________________

TO: ________________

____

Jesus is the source of my abundance...

With the Lord at my side I can accomplish anything today. All life, truth, and love are mine through His generosity.

God's Word says...

Blessed is the man
Who walks not in the counsel of the ungodly,
Nor stands in the path of sinners,
Nor sits in the seat of the scornful;
But his delight is in the law of the LORD,
And in His law he meditates day and night.
He shall be like a tree
Planted by the rivers of water,
That brings forth its fruit in its season,
Whose leaf also shall not wither;
And whatever he does shall prosper.

Psalm 1:1-3

To accept Jesus Christ as your personal Lord and Savior, pray out loud:

Heavenly Father,
I come to You in the name of Jesus. I believe in my heart that Jesus Christ is the Son of God, that He died on the Cross for my sins and was raised from the dead for my justification. I believe in my heart, and I now confess with my mouth that Jesus is Lord. Therefore, I am saved!